TABLE OF CONTENTS

CONTACTING ARLINGTON NATIONAL CEMETERY

On the Web:
http://www.arlingtoncemetery.mil

By phone:
Toll free: 1-877-907-8585
Mailing Address:
Arlington National Cemetery
Arlington, VA 22211

HOURS OF OPERATION FOR FUNERAL SERVICES

Funeral services are held Monday through Friday, except federal holidays, from 9 a.m. to 3 p.m. Saturday services are also available from 9 a.m. to 1 p.m. for services that do not require military honors. Family members and others attending the funeral should arrive at the cemetery 30 minutes prior to the scheduled service time. To request or coordinate funeral services, please call (877) 907-8585.

All in attendance must provide their own transportation for funeral services at Arlington National Cemetery. Transportation is required from the Administration Building or chapel to the final resting place, the gravesite or niche location.

HOURS OF OPERATION FOR VISITATION

The cemetery is open year-round (365 days) for visitation. Visitation hours are:
    October 1 through March 31: 8 a.m. to 5 p.m.
    April 1 through September 30: 8 a.m. to 7 p.m.

PURPOSE

This guide is to be used to obtain general information regarding policies and procedures for burial and related activities at Arlington National Cemetery. Veterans and their dependents or personal representatives can use this to assist in eligibility determination for interment (ground burial of either casketed or inurned remains) and for Columbarium/Wall inurnment (cremated remains) and to better understand the burial process at Arlington National Cemetery. The guide also contains information essential to process a future request for interment or inurnment, submit questions, issues or concerns regarding gravesites and other important information regarding cemetery procedures and regulations.

GENERAL INFORMATION

Arlington National Cemetery is a national cemetery administered by the Department of the Army. The primary mission of Arlington National Cemetery is to serve as the final resting place for the men and women who honorably served in the Armed Forces and their immediate family members. The cemetery routinely performs 20 to 30 funeral services each day.

Vision: America's premier military cemetery

- A national shrine
- A living history of freedom
- Where dignity and honor rest in solemn repose.

Mission: On behalf of the American people, lay to rest those who have served our nation with dignity and honor, treating their families with respect and compassion, and connecting guests to the rich tapestry of the cemetery's living history, while maintaining these hallowed grounds befitting the sacrifice of all those who rest here in quiet repose.

The grounds of Arlington National Cemetery honor those who have served our nation by providing a sense of beauty and peace for our guests. The rolling green hills are dotted with trees that are hundreds of years in age and complement the gardens found throughout the 624 developed acres of the cemetery. This impressive landscape serves as a tribute to the service and sacrifice of every individual laid to rest within the hallowed grounds of Arlington National Cemetery.

Maps of Arlington National Cemetery are available on our website at:

Cemetery Map: http://www.arlingtoncemetery.mil/docs/ANC_Map.pdf

ANC Explorer: http://public.mapper.army.mil/ANC/ANCWeb/PublicWMV/ancWeb.html

ESTABLISHING ELIGIBILITY

Eligibility for Interment (Ground Burial of Casketed or Cremated Remains)

Eligibility for interment at Arlington National Cemetery is verified at the time of need (at the time of death) and cannot be verified by the cemetery or accommodated before that time. However, in accordance with the 1986 Title 32 Code of Federal Regulations Part 553, section 15, the following individuals are eligible for interment (ground burial) at Arlington National Cemetery:

(a) Any active duty member of the Armed Forces (except those members serving on active duty for training only).

(b) Any retired member of the Armed Forces. A retired member of the Armed Forces, in the context of this paragraph, is a retired member of the Army, Navy, Air Force, Marine Corps, Coast Guard, or a Reserve component who has served on active duty (other than for training), is carried on an official retired list, and is entitled to receive retired pay stemming from service in the Armed Forces. If, at the time of death, a retired member of the Armed Forces is not entitled to receive retired pay stemming from his service in the Armed Forces until some future date, the retired member will not be eligible for ground burial.

(c) Any former member of the Armed Forces separated for physical disability prior to 1 October 1949 who has served on active duty (other than for training) and who would have been eligible for retirement under the provisions of 10 United States Code (U.S.C.) 1201 had that statute been in effect on the date of his separation.

(d) Any former member of the Armed Forces whose last active duty (other than for training) military service terminated honorably and who has been awarded one of the following decorations:
    (1) Medal of Honor.
    (2) Distinguished Service Cross (Air Force Cross or Navy Cross).
    (3) Distinguished Service Medal.
    (4) Silver Star.
    (5) Purple Heart.
(e) Persons who have held any of the following positions provided their last period of active duty (other than for training) as a member of the Armed Forces terminated honorably:
(1) An elective office of the United States Government.
(2) Office of the Chief Justice of the United States or of an Associate Justice of the Supreme Court of the United States.
(3) An office listed in 5 U.S.C. 5312 or 5 U.S.C. 5313.
(4) The Chief of a mission who was at any time during his/her tenure classified in class I under the provisions of Section 411 of the Act of 13 August 1946, 60 Stat. 1002, as amended (22 U.S.C. 866, 1964 ed.).
(f) Any former prisoner of war who, while a prisoner of war, served honorably in the active military, naval, or air service, whose last period of active military, naval, or air service terminated honorably and who died on or after November 30, 1993.

(1) The term "former prisoner of war" means a person who, while serving in the active military, naval, or air service, was forcibly detained or interned in line of duty—

(i) By an enemy government or its agents, or a hostile force, during a period of war; or

(ii) By a foreign government or its agents, or a hostile force, under circum stances which the Secretary of Veterans Affairs finds to have been comparable to the circumstances under which persons have generally been forcibly detained or interned by enemy governments during periods of war.

(2) The term "active military, naval, or air service" includes active duty, any period of active duty for training during which the individual concerned was disabled or died from a disease or injury incurred or aggravated in line of duty, and any period of inactive duty training during which the individual concerned was disabled or died from an injury incurred or aggravated in line of duty.

(g) The spouse, widow or widower, minor child and, at the discretion of the Secretary of the Army, an unmarried adult dependent child of any of the persons listed above. (Army Regulation 290-5 defines an adult dependent child as an adult permanently incapable of self-support because of physical or mental disability incurred before age 21.)

(1) The term "spouse" refers to a widow or widower of an eligible member, including the widow or widower of a member of the Armed Forces who was lost or buried at sea or officially determined to be permanently absent in a stat us of missing or missing in action. A surviving spouse who has remarried and whose remarriage is void, terminated by death, or dissolved by annulment or divorce by a court with basic authority to render such decrees regains eligibility for burial in Arlington National Cemetery unless it is determined that the decree of annulment or divorce was secured through fraud or collusion.

(2) An unmarried adult child may be interred in the same gravesite in which the parent has been or will be interred, provided that child was incapable of self-support up to the time of death because of physical or mental condition. At the time of death of an adult child, a request for interment will be submitted to the Executive Director, Army National Cemeteries Program, Arlington National Cemetery. The request must be accompanied by a notarized statement from an individual who has direct knowledge as to the marital status, degree of dependency of the deceased child, the name of that child's parent, and the military service upon which the burial is being requested. A certificate of a physician who has attended the decedent as to the nature and duration of the physical and/or mental disability must also accompany the request for interment.

(h) Widows or widowers of service m embers who are interred in Arlington National Cemetery as part of a group burial may be interred/inurned in the cemetery, but not in the same gravesite as the group burial.

(i) The surviving spouse, minor child, and, at the discretion of the Secretary of the Army, unmarried adult dependent child of any person already buried in Arlington. (Army Regulation 290-5 defines an adult dependent child as an adult permanently incapable of self-support because of physical or mental disability incurred before age 21.)

(j) The parents of a minor child or unmarried adult dependent child whose remains, based on the eligibility of a parent, are already buried in Arlington National Cemetery. (Army Regulation 290-5 defines an adult dependent child as an adult permanently incapable of self-support because of physical or mental disability incurred before age 21.)

Eligibility for Inurnment in the Columbarium or Niche Wall

Eligibility for inurnment at Arlington National Cemetery is verified at the time of need (at the time of death) and cannot be verified by the cemetery or accommodated before the time of need. However, in accordance with 24 United States Code 281 and Title 32 Code of Federal Regulations Part 553, section 15a, the following individuals are eligible for inurnment (Columbarium or Niche Wall) at Arlington National Cemetery:

(a) Any member of the Armed Forces who dies on active duty.

(b) Any former member of the Armed Forces who served on active duty (other than for training) and whose last service terminated honorably.

(c) Any member of a Reserve component of the Armed Forces, and any member of the Army National Guard or the Air National Guard, whose death occurs under honorable conditions while he is on active duty for training or performing full-time service; performing authorized travel to or from that duty or service; or is on authorized inactive duty training including training performed as a member of the Army National Guard or the Air National Guard. Also included are those members whose deaths occur while hospitalized or undergoing treatment at the expense of the United States for injury or disease contracted or incurred under honorable conditions while on that duty or service or performing that travel or inactive duty training.

(d) Any member of the Reserve Officers' Training Corps of the Army, Navy, or Air Force whose death occurs under honorable conditions while attending an authorized training camp or on an authorized practice cruise, performing authorized travel to or from that camp or cruise, or hospitalized or undergoing treatment at the expense of the United States for injury or disease contracted or incurred under honorable conditions while attending that camp or cruise, performing that travel, or undergoing that hospitalization or treatment at the expense of the United States.

(e) Any former prisoner of war who, while a prisoner of war, served honorably in the active military, naval, or air service, whose last period of active military, naval, or air service terminated honorably and who died on or after November 30, 1993.

(1) The term "former prisoner of war" means a person who, while serving in the active military, naval, or air service, was forcibly detained or interned in line of duty—

(i) By an enemy government or its agents, or a hostile force, during a period of war; or
(ii) By a foreign government or its agents, or a hostile force, under circum stances which the Secretary of Veterans Affairs finds to have been comparable to the circumstances under which persons have generally been forcibly detained or interned by enemy governments during periods of war.

(2) The term "active military, naval, or air service" includes active duty, any period of active duty for training during which the individual concerned was disabled or died from a disease or injury incurred or aggravated in line of duty, and any period of inactive duty training during which the individual concerned was disabled or died from an injury incurred or aggravated in line of duty.

(f) Any citizen of the United States who, during any war in which the United States has been or may hereafter be engaged, served in the Armed Forces of any government allied with the United States during that war, whose last active service terminated honorably by death or otherwise, and who was a citizen of the United States at the time of entry on such service and at the time of death.

(g) Commissioned officers, United States Coast and Geodetic Survey (now National Oceanic and

Atmospheric Administration) who die during or subsequent to the service specified in the following categories and whose last service terminated honorably:

(1) Assignment to areas of immediate military hazard.

(2) Served in the Philippine Islands on December 7, 1941.

(3) Transferred to the Department of the Army or the Department of the Navy under certain statutes.

(h) Any commissioned officer of the United States Public Health Service who served on full-time duty on or after July 29, 1945, if the service falls within the meaning of active duty for training as defined in 38 U.S.C. 101(22) or inactive duty training as defined in 38 U.S.C. 101(23) and whose death resulted from a disease or injury incurred or aggravated in line of duty. Also, any commissioned officer of the Regular or Reserve Corps of the Public Health Service who performed active service prior to July 29, 1945 in time of war; on detail for duty with the Armed Forces; or while the service was part of the military forces of the United States pursuant to Executive order of the President.

(i) Spouses, minor children and adult dependent children of the persons listed above. (Army Regulation 290-5 defines an adult dependent child as an adult permanently incapable of self-support because of physical or mental disability incurred before age 21.)

Burden of Proof in Establishing Eligibility

The next-of-kin or designated personal representative is responsible for providing the appropriate documentation to verify the veteran's eligibility for interment or inurnment. The cemetery staff may offer assistance in verifying the veteran's eligibility. However, the veteran or their spouse must be deceased (time of need) prior to the cemetery staff assisting with the verification. Verification by the cemetery staff may take time and it is recommended that the next-of-kin or designated personal representative make every effort to obtain requested eligibility documents. Documents that can be used for establishing eligibility include:

☐ Department of Defense (DD) Form 214 (all branches starting in the 1950s)
☐ War Department Adjutant General's Office (WDAGO) Form 53, 53-55 or 53-98 for Army
☐ Navy Personnel (NAVPERS) Form 553 for Navy
☐ Navy/Marine Corps (NAVMC) Form 553 (f or the Marines during the 1940s; both front and back of the forms are needed).

A Record of Service provided by the National Personnel Records Center is also acceptable to establish eligibility. The preceding list represents a partial listing of forms used during the 1940s. Some of the preceding documents do not describe the character of service. A copy of the veteran's discharge certificate, which describes the character of service as "honorable" or "under honorable conditions," will meet the characterization of service requirement.

Veterans or their designated representative who desire copies of a veteran's military records should write to:

National Personnel Records Center
Attention: Military Personnel Records
9700 Page Boulevard St. Louis, Missouri 63132-5100
Telephone: (314) 801-0800
Monday through Friday, 7:30 a.m. to 3:45 p.m.
(Closed weekends and Federal holidays)

E-mail: MPR.center@nara.gov
Status Check: mpr.status@nara.gov
Fax: (314) 801-9195
Requests may also be made online at vetrecs.archives.gov

Active-Duty Deaths: Any m ember of the Uniformed Services who dies while on active duty (other than for training) will generally have his/her affairs processed by a casualty assistance officer from his/her respective branch of service. An active duty statement from the commanding officer will be required for verification of eligibility.

Application for an Exception to the Interment/Inurnment Policy

A notarized letter requesting an exception to policy should be submitted to the Executive Director, Army National Cemeteries Program, Arlington National Cemetery, Arlington, VA 22211. A request for an exception to policy will not be considered until the death of the individual. A written request for exception must contain the following information:

(a) Name of the deceased.

(b) Reason(s) why the deceased should be favorably considered for an exception to policy. All relevant information regarding military service or service to the nation should be included. All documentation of service should be included (i.e., DD Form 214, award certificates, orders, etc.)

(c) If interment is to be in the same gravesite as someone already interred, provide the full name of the previously interred person and the section/gravesite number where interred, if known. Include the relationship of the deceased to the previously interred person.

(d) A point of contact with daytime and evening telephone numbers is required.

(e) The Next of Kin or personal representative (assigned in writing by formal designation) will read and sign the public disclosure form and forward it with the exception request. Copies of the public disclosure form are available on the web at www.arlingtoncemetery.mil, in hard copy from the front desk at the Administration Building, or by telephone (877) 907-8585.

(f) Notarized signature of the requestor.

Circumstances may require additional information. Requests that would displace an otherwise eligible veteran will require Secretary of the Army or higher approval and requires a longer processing time for rendering of a final decision.

Capital Crimes Prohibition

As provided by 38 United States Code Section 2411 (38 U.S.C. § 2411), certain persons may not be interred, inurned, or memorialized at Arlington National Cemetery. The persons statutorily ineligible for interment, inurnment, and memorialization are indentified as follows:

(1) A person who has been convicted of a federal capital crime and whose conviction is final (other than a person whose sentence was commuted by the President).

(2) A person who has been convicted of a State capital crime and whose conviction is final (other than a person whose sentence was commuted by the Governor of a state).

(3) A person who—

(a) was found (by the Secretary of the Army) to have committed a Federal capital crime or a State capital crime, but

(b) has not been convicted of such crime by reason of such person not being available for trial due to death or flight to avoid prosecution.

The term "Federal capital crime" means an offense under Federal law for which a sentence of imprisonment for life or the death penalty may be imposed.

The term "State capital crime" means, under State law, the willful, deliberate, or premeditated unlawful killing of another human being for which a sentence of imprisonment for life or the death penalty may be imposed.

In order to comply with Federal law; Army policy is that all primary next of kin are required to declare that 38 U.S.C. § 2411 is not applicable, prior to interment/inurnment of their family member at Arlington National Cemetery.

Eligibility for Interment at a Department of Veterans Affairs (VA) National Cemetery

Individuals found not specifically eligible for burial at Arlington National Cemetery, may be eligible for burial at a Department of Veterans Affairs National Cemetery. For burial eligibility or information, contact the local VA Office. The nearest VA National Cemetery can be found on the web at: http://www.va.gov, by phone at 1-800-535-1117, or by mail at:

US Department of Veterans Affairs
National Cemetery Administration (402B2)
810 Vermont Avenue, NW
Washington, DC 20420

AT THE TIME OF NEED/TIME OF DEATH

Arranging an Interment (Ground Burial of Casketed or Cremated Remains)

Upon the death of the veteran or veteran' s spouse, the surviving spouse or persona l representative should contact a local funeral home to arrange for any desired services in the hometown. The surviving spouse, personal representative, or the funeral director should telephone the Arlington National Cemetery's Customer Service Call Center at (877) 907-8585 to arrange for the interment/inurnment service.

An individual case number will be assigned and a cemetery representative will call the point of contact to establish eligibility. Before scheduling the service, the cemetery staff will need to determine the eligibility of the deceased in accordance with Arlington National Cemetery interment eligibility criteria. Upon verification of eligibility, the cemetery staff will reserve the necessary ceremonial resources and schedule the interment. Any documents requested by the cemetery staff to confirm eligibility can be digitally faxed to the cemetery at telephone number (571) 256-3334 or emailed to Arlingtoncemetery.isb@mail.mil and must include the case number provided by the Customer Service Call Center. Please note Arlington National Cemetery will not respond to other inquiries via this email box.

Arranging an Inurnment in the Columbarium, Niche Wall or Designated Cemetery Unmarked Area

Arranging for an inurnment service is the same as for arranging for an interment (ground burial) service. The urn (no greater in size than 13" high x 10" wide x 9" deep) containing the cremated remains must be made of a durable material tightly sealed and hand carried by the family or delivered by a local funeral home. The cemetery does not accept cremated remains sent via US Postal Services or common carrier.

Please note, partial (or split) remains will not be accepted for burial. Cremated remains interred or inurned at Arlington National Cemetery must be delivered with a Death Certificate and a Certificate of Cremation.

Columbarium and wall niches are designed to accommodate two receptacles (e.g., for a veteran and eligible spouse). Accordingly, it is important that these dimensions are considered when purchasing an urn (receptacle). If a second inurnment is anticipated, both receptacles must fit within these dimensions therefore it is recommended that the receptacle be no larger than 13" high x 5" wide x 9" deep.

When the caisson is being provided to transport cremated remains, for ground burial or inurnment in either the Columbarium or Niche Wall, the single receptacle, in addition to a folded American flag (5' x 9 ½'), must fit within a confined area measuring 11" in height, 13" in width, and 16" in length. For the purpose of the ceremony and placement on the caisson, the receptacle should utilize no more than half of the total space available.

Cemetery Unmarked Area

Cremated remains of any person eligible for inurnment at Arlington National Cemetery may be interred in the designated unmarked area. Cremated remains must either be interred in a biodegradable container or placed directly in to the ground without a container. Scattering of remains at this site or any other location at Arlington National Cemetery is unauthorized. No headstone or marker (government issued, personally purchased or memorial marker) is placed for a person choosing this method of interment and no additional gravesite, niche, or memorial marker in a Memorial Area is authorized. Once an eligible veteran is interred in this manner in the unmarked section, any additional eligible family members (spouse) must be interred in the Unmarked Area as well. Arlington National Cemetery maintains records of all persons buried in the unmarked area.

Interment/Inurnment Costs

Arlington National Cemetery does not charge fees for an interment or inurnment at the cemetery. The only potential costs to the estate of the deceased are for private headstone monuments or vaults. The next-of-kin may elect to have a private headstone monument (depending on the availability of gravesites in sections of the cemetery where private headstone monuments are permitted) erected in lieu of using a government-provided headstone. Please note, the availability of gravesites in the older sections of the cemetery is limited. Additionally, the next-of-kin may elect to provide a private vault as an outside container other than the standard government provided grave liner.

Government grave liners are made of reinforced concrete that surrounds the casket. After the committal service, the casket is lowered into the government liner and the concrete lid is placed on top. The purpose of the government liner is to protect the grave from sinking. It is not designed to protect the casket from the elements. A government liner is provided at no cost to the family.

A burial vault is made of reinforced concrete or other materials such as steel or bronze. Burial vaults come with a variety of special linings and may be sold with a warranty. The purpose of the burial vault is to

11

protect the casket for some period of time and prevent the grave from sinking. Burial vaults are sold by funeral homes and not provided free of charge by the cemetery. If a family elects to purchase a burial vault, then the cemetery will not provide the free government liner.

The overall purpose of both is to prevent ground sinkage as the casket naturally deteriorates over time. The outer burial container helps to prevent the grave from sinking but neither grave liners nor burial vaults are designed to prevent the eventual decomposition of human remains, or entirely prevent water, dirt, or other debris from penetrating into a casket.

All costs associated with preparation of the remains, casket or urn, and shipping of the remains to the Washington, D.C. area are at the expense of the estate, unless the deceased was on active duty with a branch of the Armed Forces. Please check with your local VA and Social Security Administration office to determine if any benefits are available from either or both agencies.

Assignment of Gravesites/Niches

Assignments of gravesites and niches are without regard to military rank, race, color, creed, or gender of the qualifying service member. At the time of need (time of death of the eligible individual), the family may request a specific burial location within the cemetery, close to other family members interred or inurned within the cemetery or a significant memorial or marker. The cemetery will accept and consider each request on a case-by-case basis.

MILITARY FUNERAL HONORS

The military funeral honors provided at Arlington National Cemetery differ from those provided in other national cemeteries.

Enlisted Personnel: Military funeral honors can be provided by the decedent's branch of service. The cemetery staff will arrange for the military funeral honors when military funeral honors are requested. The honors will include service specific casket team (also referred to as body bearers or pallbearers), firing party, and a bugler. Additional honors may be available for certain senior non-commissioned officers (pay grade of E-9) depending upon the branch of service. A military chaplain may be scheduled by the cemetery staff, unless the family minister is desired and provided by the next-of-kin or the funeral home.

Please note, in accordance with guidance from the Secretary of the Army (SecArmy Memorandum Subject: Funeral Honors at Arlington National Cemetery for Soldiers Who Die as a Result of Wounds Received in Action, dated 02 January 2009), all service members who die from wounds received as a result of enemy action and are being interred, inurned or memorialized at Arlington National Cemetery are eligible to receive full military funeral honors.

Commissioned and Warrant Officers: In addition to the military funeral honors provided above, the caisson, band, and escort troops may be scheduled by the cemetery staff, if requested. The caparisoned (riderless) horse is used only for Army and Marine Colonels and above. For General/Flag Officers of the Navy, Coast Guard, and Marines, the Minute Guns are provided. For General/Flag Officers of the Army, Navy, Air Force, Coast Guard, and Marines, the Gun Salute is provided.

If the temperature is below 32 degrees Fahrenheit, then all elements of the band may not be available to perform. A modified band will then provide the honors. Additionally, certain weather conditions may make it unsafe for the horses pulling the caisson to support a funeral service.

Certified active military service: Former members of a group that has been certified as active military service for the purpose of receiving veteran benefits, under Section 401 of Public Law 95-202, are therefore entitled to inurnment in the Colum barium and are also deemed entitled to military funeral honors. Military funeral honors will be provided such honors when requested. The honors will include casket bearers (pallbearers), firing party, and a bugler. A military chaplain may be scheduled by the cemetery staff unless the family minister is desired and provided by the next-of-kin or the funeral home.

Dependents with no military service: The cemetery staff will arrange for casket bearers (pallbearers) and the family may request a military chaplain.

TYPES OF MILITARY FUNERALS

Funeral Escorts (Standard Honors): Enlisted service members interred/inurned at Arlington National Cemetery will receive honors provided by the decedent's branch of service. These honors include:

- A casket team (body bearers / pallbearers);
- A firing party; and
- A bugler

Additionally, all branches of the armed services may use the caisson, if available, for service members who have reached the senior non-commissioned officer (pay grade of E-9). The cemetery staff will make arrangements for military funeral honors when requested by the next-of-kin or representative. A military chaplain may also be requested.

Please note, in accordance with guidance from the Secretary of the Army (SecArmy Memorandum, SUBJECT: Funeral Honors at Arlington National Cemetery for Soldiers Who Die as a Result of Wounds Received in Action, dated 02 January 2009), enlisted members who die as a result of wounds received in action and are being interred/inurned at Arlington National Cemetery are eligible to receive full military funeral honors, to include an escort platoon, a colors team, a band, and a caisson section.

Funeral Escorts (Full Military Funeral Honors): In addition to the standard military funeral honors, those eligible for full military funeral honors at Arlington National Cemetery may also receive:

- An escort platoon (size varies according to the rank of the deceased)
- A military band

Additionally, those eligible for full military funeral honors at Arlington National Cemetery may use the caisson, if available. Officers in the rank of colonel and above in the Army and the Marine Corps may be provided a caparisoned (riderless) horse, if available. General/flag officers may receive a cannon salute (17 guns for a four-star general, 15 for a three-star, 13 for a two-star, 11 for a one-star), if available. The President of the United States is entitled to a 21-gun salute, while other high state officials receive 19 guns.

Armed Forces Honors: Armed Forces Honors are the same as a full military funeral honors funeral, except that escort platoons from each of the services participate. These funerals are reserved for the President of the United States (as commander-in-chief), Secretary of Defense, Chairman of the Joint Chiefs of Staff or officers granted multiple-service command.

Military spouses and family members: When a spouse or other dependent of a current or former member of the Armed Forces is buried at Arlington, the military service in which the primary party served will provide a casket team and a chaplain. No other military funeral honors will be rendered unless the spouse also served in the military.

Sequence of Events for Military Funeral Honors Service at Arlington National Cemetery:

- The caisson or hearse arrives at gravesite, everyone presents arms (renders a salute).
- Casket team secures the casket, non-commissioned officer-in-charge (NCOIC), officer-in-charge (OIC), and chaplain salute.
- Chaplain leads the way to gravesite, followed by casket team.
- Casket team sets down the casket and secures the flag.
- The NCOIC ensures the flag is stretched out and level, and centered over the casket.
- The family will be seated.
- NCOIC backs away and the chaplain, military or civilian, will perform the service.
- At conclusion of interment service and before benediction, a gun salute is fired for those eligible (i.e., general officers).
- Chaplain concludes his service and backs away, NCOIC steps up to the casket.
- The cemetery representative will ask all family members to rise for honors.
- The NCOIC presents arms to initiate the rifle volley.
- Rifle volley complete, bugler plays "Taps."
- Family will be asked to be seated.
- Casket-team leader starts to fold the flag.
- Flag fold complete, and the flag is passed to the NCOIC, OIC.
- Casket team leaves gravesite.
- NCOIC, OIC either presents the flag to the next-of-kin, or if there is a military chaplain on site he will present the flag to the chaplain, and then the chaplain will present to the next-of-kin.
- For veterans of the Army, Air Force, Navy and Coast Guard, an Arlington Lady presents a card of condolences to the next-of-kin on behalf of their service chief.
- Chaplain/family clergy will extend condolences.
- Cemetery representative announces that the service is concluded.

OTHER GENERAL BURIAL INFORMATION

Burial Flags

Burial flags used for military honors at Arlington National Cemetery measure 5' x 9 ½'. Most funeral homes will obtain the US Flag on behalf of the veteran's family. Requests for a burial flag must be made at the time of need (time of death). Burial flags may be obtained from VA regional offices and most U.S. post offices by completing VA Form 21-2008, Application for United States Flag for Burial Purposes, and submitting it with a copy of the veteran's discharge papers at either of the locations.

Gravesite Markers/Niche Covers

Government Headstone/Niche Cover: The government will provide at no cost to the estate of the deceased an upright, white marble headstone or white niche cover. The cemetery staff at Arlington will place the order, which goes to the National Cemetery Administration, which is part of the Department of Veterans Affairs. The order for the headstone or niche cover will include the appropriate inscription and choice of emblem of belief.

Headstones, provided by the government, are ordered after the day of interment. The next-of-kin will review the proposed stone text prior to the date of interment and then agree and finalize the order on the day of the interment at the chapel or administrative building at Arlington National Cemetery.

Upright marble stones (13x24x4) generally contain eleven lines of text with or without an emblem of belief. Headstones are ordered from the Veteran's Administration and follow standard guidelines. Generally, the stone can accommodate 13 characters and spaces per name line, 15 characters and spaces on all others. A veteran's government headstone must contain name, rank, date of birth and date of death. Other lines can include com bat service and significant awards. An additional inscription can be used to show a term of endearment or reference (e.g. Loving Father, Husband and Son).

Niche granite or marble covers (15 ¾ x 11 ¼ x ¼) generally contain 11 lines including a religious emblem and have 11 characters on the name line, 13 on all others except the 11th line which only contains 10 characters or spaces.

While the next-of-kin does not order the government headstone/niche cover for placement in Arlington National Cemetery, he or she can check on the status of the order by calling, toll-free 1-877-907-8585, between 7:45 a.m. and 3:45 p.m. Eastern Time. The next-of-kin as listed on the record of interment will receive a post card via the U.S. Postal Service when the headstone arrives and is placed.

Lithochrome Policy

The first headstones at Arlington National Cemetery were simple white headstones with the personal information and gravesite number etched into the stone. Later, lithochrome (a special type of water-resistant paint applied to headstones/markers that darkens all of the letters) was introduced to make the inscriptions easier to read. Over time, depending on location, conditions and the specific lithochrome paint used, the blackening fades. The fading occurs in a very nonuniform way, both within a particular headstone and across a section. Additionally, there are sections that were traditionally non-lithochromed where lithochromed headstones have been introduced. The current policy states that headstones will be ordered consistent with the character of the section in which they are to be placed.

(a) Headstones ordered for sections 54, 59, 6 0, and 64, as well as niche covers for the Columbarium and Niche Wall, will be lithochromed.

(b) Lithochrome will not be used when ordering headstones for any other section.

(c) Headstones and niche covers will only be replaced because of fading, if requested by the immediate next-of-kin as listed on the original record of interment.

(d) Any new sections or sections not listed above will not have lithochrome.

Private Headstone Markers

Certain sections of the cemetery have been specified as sections where private headstone markers can be placed. Private headstone markers placed in the cemetery are subject to approval prior to installation. In accordance with the Code of Federal Regulations (32 CFR Part 553.21), the marker will be o f simple design, dignified, and appropriate to a military cemetery. Additionally, the Department of the Army is not liable for the maintenance of or damage to private markers.

(a) The erection of headstone markers at private expense to m ark graves in lieu of government headstones and markers is permitted only in sections of Arlington National Cemetery in which private headstone markers were authorized as of 1 January 1947. These markers will be of simple design, dignified, and appropriate to a military cemetery. The name of the person(s) or the name of an organization, fraternity, or society responsible for the purchase and erection of the marker will not be permitted on the marker or anywhere else in the cemetery. More specific and detailed information can be provided upon request.

(b) Except as may be authorized for marking group burials, ledger markers of freestanding cross design, narrow shafts, mausoleums, or over-ground vaults are prohibited.

Grave liner, Urn Liner and Burial Vault

Grave and urn liners are concrete containers in which caskets or urns are placed. The government will provide a grave or urn liner for an initial casketed interment or inurnment at no cost. If the previous interment was without a grave liner or vault and the subsequent interment is on top of the previous interment, the government will not provide a grave liner. Due to space limitation in some sections of the cemetery, a government grave liner cannot always be used. The government reserves the right to use a plastic liner in the place of a concrete liner when appropriate.

Grave liners are used by the government to reduce the amount of settling/sinkage of the gravesite subsequent to the interment. Grave liners are not intended to protect the casket. If the next of kin desires to ensure protection of the casket, a burial vault may be purchased at no expense to Arlington National Cemetery or the government.

Urn liners are used in some sections of the cemetery. Urn liners may be used when an urn is being interred in the ground. The characteristics are similar to that of a grave liner and the dimensions are 14" high, 14" wide and 14" long.

Burial Vaults

A burial vault is made of reinforced concrete or other materials such as steel or bronze. Burial vaults come with a variety of special linings and may be sold with a warranty. The purpose of the burial vault is to protect the casket for some period of time and prevent the grave from sinking. Burial vaults are sold by funeral homes and not provided free of charge by the cemetery. If a family elects to purchase a burial vault, then the cemetery will not provide the free government liner.

The overall purpose of both is to prevent the ground from caving in as the casket naturally deteriorates over time. The outer burial container helps to prevent the grave from sinking but neither grave liners nor burial vaults are designed to prevent the eventual decomposition of human remains, or entirely prevent water, dirt, or other debris from penetrating into a casket.

AFTER THE TIME OF NEED

Locating a Gravesite or Niche

To locate the gravesite or niche in the Columbarium/Wall for a relative or friend, you may use the Department of Veterans Affairs' National Gravesite Locator that can be found on the web at: http://gravelocator.cem.va.gov.

You may call the Arlington National Cemetery's Customer Service Call Center using the toll-free telephone number (877) 907-8585 or visit the information desk in the Visitors Center. Except for Christmas Day, the Visitors Center is open every day of the year. The hours open to the public are:

8 a.m. to 5 p.m. from October 1 through March 31

8 a.m. to 7 p.m. from April 1 through September 30

Gravesite Maintenance after Interment

Gravesites are filled and leveled after each interment. As the soil compacts and settles at the gravesite, sinkage may occur, especially during the first year after the interment. However, the Cemetery staff monitors this closely and quickly corrects these situations. Gravesites are sodded in the spring (normally March through May) or in the fall (normally September through November). Forms are available in the Visitors Center for you to express any specific concerns you may have regarding your loved one's gravesite condition.

Vehicle Passes for Gravesite Visitation

Permanent Pass: A permanent pass is issued to the next-of-kin at the time of the interment or inurnment. Permanent passes are available to spouses, parents, children and siblings of the deceased. An application for a permanent pass is available at the Administration Building, from the Arlington National Cemetery Visitor's Center and on the Arlington National Cemetery website (www.arlingtoncemetery.mil), or you may write for an application to: Arlington National Cemetery, Arlington, VA 22211. Completed pass request form s can be emailed to ANCParking@conus.army.mil.

Temporary Pass: A temporary pass may be issued to additional family and friends of the deceased. You may request a temporary pass upon your visit to Arlington National Cemetery. To request a pass, you may visit the Customer Service Desk located in the Visitors Center. The staff will issue a temporary pass and will provide the gravesite location and a map to the gravesite. The pass is only good for one visit, but additional passes can be requested upon subsequent visits. To access the Visitors Center, you should park in the paid parking facility (the first 30 minutes of parking are free).

Vehicle passes may only be used to visit specific grave sites and is not to be used to park near and tour Arlington National Cemetery, i.e. the Kennedy Grave Site, Tomb of the Unknowns and the Lee Mansion.

Floral Tributes at Gravesites

- Fresh cut flowers may be placed on gravesites at any time. Arlington National Cemetery provides portable cones for flowers that public may use. These cones can be found throughout the cemetery in centralized stone containers.
- Artificial flowers may be placed on gravesites from October 10 through April 15.
- The government does not assume any responsibility for damaged or missing flower arrangements.
- Planting of flowers, shrubs, etc. is prohibited.
- Potted plants are permitted during the period 7 days before and 7 days after Easter.
- Wreaths are permitted during the holiday season (from 1 Dec until mid-January).
- Floral items will be removed from the gravesites as soon as they become faded and unsightly.
- Prohibited decorations include: statues, vigil lights, flags, glass objects of any nature, and any type of commemorative items and are not permitted on gravesites—except for U.S. flags placed on the gravesites by government employees for Memorial Day.
- Floral items and other types of decorations are not to be secured to the headstone or marker.
- Flowers may be placed at the bottom of a column at the niche wall or in the Columbarium.

Permanent Flower Containers

Permanent flower containers that are placed below ground level and have telescoping flower vases can be privately purchased and are permitted if placed in the ground by the cemetery staff. The government does not assume any responsibility for damaged or missing flower containers.

To arrange placement once a permanent flower container is purchased, please contact the Consolidated Customer Service Center at (877) 907-8585 and a representative will contact you regarding the process for final placement.

Living Gift Process

Individuals requesting to proffer a gift of a living tree or plant to Arlington National Cemetery must do so in writing to the Executive Director, Arlington National Cemetery, Arlington VA 22211. The proffer should include the details of the gift, the estimated value of the gift, and contact information of the individual making the proffer. If approved, the on-site horticulturalist will coordinate with the individual offering the gift for final details and arrangements for acceptance.

Commemorative Memorial Markers

The placement of commemorative monuments in Arlington National Cemetery takes away land that might otherwise be suitable to fulfill Arlington National Cemetery's primary mission-burial and memorialization of deceased military veterans and their eligible family members. Therefore, in accordance with Title 32 Code of Federal Regulations Part 553, commemorative memorial monuments may only be placed in Arlington National Cemetery after they are authorized by a joint or concurrent resolution of Congress.

As a general matter, commemorative monuments which are authorized by Congress for placement must be submitted to the Commission of Fine Arts for advice and comment prior to acting upon or approving the plans and designs for the monument. Additionally, although not specifically required, parties seeking to place commemorative monuments in Arlington National Cemetery are encouraged to discuss their plans with the Commission of Fine Arts, and the State Historic Preservation Office for specific historical areas of the cemetery, prior to seeking Congressional authorization.

Disinterment Procedures

Burials at Arlington National Cemetery are considered final. Requests for disinterment of an individual interred/inurned at Arlington National Cemetery must be submitted in writing in accordance with the Code of Federal Regulations (32 CFR Part 553). Please note, disinterment is an exception that is only approved for those requestors whose facts merit extraordinary circumstances and if approved is accomplished without expense to the United States Government. A request must include the following requirements:

(a) A notarized letter stating the cogent reason for the disinterment request with the name of the interred/inurned individual. The request should be sent to the Executive Director, Attn: Disinterment, Arlington National Cemetery, Arlington, VA 22211. The notarized request must also contain the following additional documents:

(b) A notarized statement from all close living relatives (parents, siblings and children) of the interred individual, stating they impose no objection to the proposed disinterment.

(c) A notarized sworn statement from a third party who knows those who have provided the statements and attests to the fact that the documents enclosed include all the living close family relatives.

Public Wreath Laying At The Tomb Of The Unknown Soldier

School and civic organizations coming to visit Arlington National Cemetery can request to lay a wreath at the Tomb of the Unknown Soldier. A representative of the requesting organization must submit a request in writing to Arlington National Cemetery, Attn: Public Wreath Ceremonies, Arlington, VA 22211 on organizational letterhead.

The sender should indicate on the outside of the envelope that it is a "wreath-laying request." In order to adequately schedule a request, the letter should include:

(a) When the group is visiting;

(b) Group schedule limitations;

(c) Complete contact information in case further questions arise.

The Arlington National Cemetery Public Wreath Coordinator will contact the sender to make further arrangements and provide further instructions. Requests must be in writing; Arlington National Cemetery cannot accept fax, e-mail or telephone requests. Tour bus and visiting bus access to the Memorial Amphitheater and Tomb of the Unknowns is authorized by exception only and not authorized prior to 4:00 p.m., Monday through Friday due to funeral services.

Commemorative Flag Flying Requests

Individuals may request a flag to be flown over the Tomb of the Unknowns at Arlington National Cemetery. The requests must be submitted in writing to the address below and include the following:

- The sender's name, address, telephone number, and email address (if available)

- One U.S. Flag (footage sizes 3X5, 4X6, 5X8, or 6X10 - are accepted)

- A self-addressed return package with pre-paid postage for returning the flag to the sender

- Arlington National Cemetery cannot accept cash, money order, or checks for return postage. We accept FEDEX, USPS, UPS, First Class/Priority mail. If you choose to ship UPS, please ensure that your pre-printed return shipping label includes the shipping cost as well as the charges for picking up the package from Arlington National Cemetery. UPS will not pick packages unless the pick -up costs are included when the return label is scanned.

- The name of the person or organization for which the flag will be flown. If the individual is/was military, please provide the service member's rank and service component.

Please allow 3 weeks from the date the flag is received to be flown and returned. Arlington National Cemetery is not responsible for the loss or damage to any flag that is mailed. Your returned flag will be accompanied by a certificate with the name of the person or organization for which the flag was flown verifying the date the flag was flown at Arlington.

Written requests should be sent to:
Arlington National Cemetery, C/O: Commemorative Flag Flying Request, Arlington, VA 22211-5003

FREQUENTLY ASKED QUESTIONS

1. What documents do I need to provide verification of eligibility for interment (in-ground burial of casketed or cremated remains)?

Answer: For decorated honorably discharged veterans, a copy of the last discharge document and a copy of the order awarding the decoration (if the decoration is not listed on the discharge document) is required. For former prisoners of war, a copy of the last discharge document and an official document that confirms the former POW status.

-For active duty personnel, an active duty statement is required.

-For veterans retired from active duty, no documentation is required unless your military retirement has been combined with your civil service retirement; a copy of your retirement order and last discharge document is required.

-For veterans retired from the Reserve Component, a copy of a discharge document that verifies active military service performed (other than for training).

-For those veterans who have held Executive Level I and II positions in the federal government and/or federal elective office, a copy of the last discharge document is required.

24

2. What documents do I need to provide verification of eligibility for inurnment of cremated remains in the Columbarium?

Answer: For honorably discharged veterans, a copy of the last discharge document will be required. For those who are serving on active duty, an active duty statement will be required. For those who are retired from active duty, no document will be required. If your military retirement has been combined with your civil service retirement, a discharge document will be required. For those who are retired from the Reserve Component, a copy of the last discharge document which describes the active service (other than for training) performed will be required.

3. What must I do to make arrangements for the interment or inurnment of myself, my spouse, or my dependent?

Answer: Arlington National Cemetery does not make prearrangements or reservations before the time of death/time of need. However, at the time of need (time of death), the surviving spouse or parent of the child should go to the local funeral home to make arrangements for any desired funeral services in your area. A funeral director should telephone Arlington National Cemetery to make burial arrangements using the toll-free Consolidated Customer Service Center (877) 907-8585. Any required documents should be provided to the funeral director. After calling and receiving a case file number, please fax or email scheduling documentation only, which is requested for establishing eligibility, using one of the contact methods below.

Please include the case number in the subject of your communications. [Example: Subject: CASE NUMBER: #####]

--Fax Number: (571) 256-3334

--Email Address: Arlingtoncemetery.isb@mail.mil

4. If I am cremated, can my next-of-kin arrange for the interment/inurnment without using the funeral home?

Answer: Yes. Your next-of-kin or personal representative can call the Consolidated Customer Service Center at the toll-free number (877) 907-8585 to receive a case number and schedule the service.

5. How does the casket or urn get to Arlington National Cemetery from where I live?

Answer: Generally, funeral directors arrange for the shipment of casketed remains through a commercial airline. Your local funeral director will contact a funeral home in the Washington, D.C. metropolitan area to arrange for the pickup of the casket at the airport. The receiving funeral home will store the casket until the day of the scheduled service. On the day of the service, the casket will be taken by the receiving funeral home to the cemetery for the interment service. All costs associated with the shipping and storage of the remains are incurred by the next-of-kin. For active duty personnel only, costs incurred are borne by the appropriate military branch of service. For cremated remains, the urn can be hand-carried to Arlington National Cemetery or shipped to a local funeral director for delivery to Arlington.

6. What is the cost to the family to have a family member interred/inurned in Arlington National Cemetery?

Answer: Arlington National Cemetery does not charge for the services provided by the cemetery. However, if the next-of-kin desires a private headstone marker/monument or a vault (in lieu of a government headstone or grave liner), the family of the deceased incurs all costs associated with the private monument or vault. Arrangements for the private headstone marker/monument and/or the vault are the responsibility of the next-of-kin. There is no charge for a gravesite, for the excavation required to open the grave, for the setup of the gravesite, or for the closing of the gravesite. There is no charge for the government headstone or government grave liner.

7. How do I arrange for the military funeral honors, a service at the chapel, coordinate for a military chaplain, or pallbearers?

Answer: The cemetery staff will advise the next-of-kin or funeral director of the available military funeral honors and casket team (pallbearers) and will schedule them for the service. At the time of scheduling for the burial service, the cemetery staff can provide a military chaplain and schedule a service at the chapel. The next-of-kin or funeral director does not have to contact the military directly to arrange for full honors for burial services at Arlington National Cemetery. Please be aware, the most important factors impacting the scheduling of the date of service are the availability of a caisson, the chapel, and a chaplain. To schedule a service, please call Arlington National Cemetery Customer Service at 877-907-8585.

8. What military funeral honors are provided at Arlington National Cemetery for the interment or inurnment service?

Answer: Interment/inurnment services and military funeral honors are provided on a first-come, first-served basis. The following honors are available, but can be modified if the family does not desire part or all of the available honors:

- Enlisted Personnel: Military funeral honors will be provided by the appropriate military branch of service, to include pallbearers, firing party, and a bugler. The cemetery staff will schedule the honors and support. A military chaplain can be scheduled, when requested, or the family minister may be provided by the next-of-kin or funeral director.

- Officers (Commissioned and Warrant): In addition to the military funeral honors and support provided for enlisted personnel, the caisson, band and escort troops can be scheduled by the cemetery staff, when requested. The riderless (caparisoned) horse is used for Army and Marine Colonels and higher. For Flag Officers (Navy, Coast Guard, and Marines), the Minute Guns are provided. For Flag Officers (Army, Navy, Coast Guard, and Marines), the Gun Salute is provided

- Aviation personnel: Each military service has specific rules and regulations regarding flyovers at military funerals and should be addressed/requested when scheduling the service.

- Dependents with no military service: The appropriate military branch of service will provide casket team (body bearers/ pallbearers). A military chaplain will be scheduled, if requested, or the family minister may be provided by the next-of-kin or funeral director.

9. What is the difference between a grave liner and a vault?

Answer: A grave liner is a concrete container in which the casket is lowered. It is used by the government for grounds maintenance purposes in that it reduces the settling of the soil, which compacts significantly during the first year following a burial. A vault is a privately purchased sealed container which protects a casket from environmental decay.

Government grave liners are made of reinforced concrete and surround the casket. After the burial service, the casket is lowered into the government liner and the concrete lid is placed on top. The purpose of the government liner is to protect the grave from sinking. It is not designed to protect the casket from the elements. A government liner is provided at no cost to the family.

A burial vault is made of reinforced concrete or other materials such as steel or bronze. Burial vaults come with a variety of special linings and may be sold with a warranty. The purpose of the burial vault is to protect the casket for some period of time and prevent the grave from sinking. Burial vaults are sold by funeral homes and not provided free of charge by the cemetery. If a family elects to purchase a burial vault, then the cemetery will not provide the free government liner.

The overall purpose of both is to prevent the ground from caving in as the casket naturally deteriorates over time. The outer burial container helps to prevent the grave from sinking but neither grave liners nor burial vaults are designed to prevent the eventual decomposition of human remains, or entirely prevent water, dirt, or other debris from penetrating into a casket.

10. If my spouse or dependent child should predecease me, can they be buried before I am buried?

Answer: Yes. However, as the qualifying veteran, you will be required to sign a statement that certifies that you will be interred/inurned in the same gravesite/niche upon your demise/death.

11. If I am the qualifying veteran and my first spouse is interred/inurned in Arlington National Cemetery and I remarry, can my second spouse also be interred/inurned in the same gravesite/niche to be occupied by me?

Answer: Yes, if you are the qualifying veteran. The qualifying veteran is the person on whose military service the eligibility for the first interment/inurnment is based. If you should predecease your second spouse, your second spouse will retain eligibility for interment/inurnment-as long as the second spouse second spouse is unmarried at the time of his/her death. Columbarium and Niche Wall niches are 13" high x 10" wide x 18" in depth and therefore can generally only accommodate two urns. These dimensions must be considered when more than one urn is anticipated to be placed in the niche. Urns being placed in the Columbarium or the Niche Wall should be of a size that will fit into the dimensions of 13x10X18.

12. Can I have a chapel service at Joint Base Myer-Henderson Hall?

Answer: Yes. Chapel services, if requested, can be scheduled by the cemetery staff at the time that burial arrangements are made. The chapel is scheduled on a first-come, first-served basis. The chapel service is conducted prior to going to the gravesite/niche for the interment/inurnment.

13. Can we use our family minister for the chapel service and at the gravesite?

Answer: Yes. However, your family minister must keep the service within the scheduled time frames in order to avoid adversely affecting the start of the next chapel service. If a long chapel service is anticipated, it should be conducted in the family church or at the funeral home.

14. If I am cremated, can I still be buried in the ground?

Answer: Yes. If you are eligible for interment (ground burial), the cremated remains may be casketed. Ground burial can be used for both caskets and urns.

15. If I am cremated, what military funeral honors are provided?

Answer: There is no distinction in the military funeral honors provided for a casketed or cremated remains.

16. Is there a special container required for interment or inurnment or cremated remains?

Answer: Yes. The heavy plastic container provided by most crematories is acceptable for ground burial or for inurnment in the Columbarium or Wall.

Cardboard containers will not be accepted for placement in a niche, but can be accepted for burial of cremated remains in the ground. Columbarium and Niche Wall niches are 13" high x 10" wide x 18" in depth and therefore can generally only accommodate two urns. These dimensions must be considered when more than one urn is anticipated to be placed in the niche. Urns being placed in the Columbarium or the Niche Wall should be of a size that will fit into the dimensions of 13x10X18.

17. What is needed on the day of the service?

Answer: Family members and others attending the funeral of the deceased should arrive at the cemetery in their private vehicles or in vehicles provided by the funeral home. These vehicles will be needed to go to the gravesite or the Columbarium for the services. The cemetery does not provide transportation or wheelchairs.

For interment or inurnment of cremated remains, you should arrive with the urn, a death certificate, a cremation certificate, and a burial flag if military funeral honors are being provided to the veteran. For casketed remains, the funeral home will provide the hearse, the casketed remains (flag draped, if a veteran), and a transfer permit (if crossing state lines).

18. How long is the wait until the service is conducted?

Answer: Scheduling of services may take from several weeks to several months, depending upon volume of services, family desires, and specific military funeral honors to be rendered. In rare circumstances, scheduling may occur more quickly. It should be noted that the availability of the chapel (if requested), availability of a military chaplain (if requested), and the military funeral honors to be rendered (especially if the caisson is to be used) are the normal causes for delays in scheduling the service.

19. Can I provide a tip or gratuity to an Arlington National Cemetery employee?

Answer: No. Law and regulation prohibit government employees from accepting a tip or gratuity of any kind.

20. Can I cremate a pet and place the remains with a pet owner or spread the cremated remains over the pet owner's grave?

Answer: No. Arlington National Cemetery cannot allow pets (cremated or otherwise) to be placed within the cemetery.

21. Who are the Arlington Ladies?

Answer: In 1948, the wife of the Chief of Staff of the United States Air Force, Hoyt Vandenberg, formed a group from the Officer's Wives Club to attend Air Force funerals.

In 1972, General Creighton Abrams wife, Julia, founded the Army's version of the group.

In 1985, the Navy also followed suit by creating a group of their own. The Marines do not officially have a group as they send a representative of the Marine Commandant to every funeral. Today, the Air Force, Army, Navy and Coast Guard all have Arlington Ladies who perform similar volunteer duties at Arlington National Cemetery for members of their respective services, attending services for all veterans.

Since 1973, the Arlington Ladies have ensured that no Soldier – old or young – is ever buried alone.

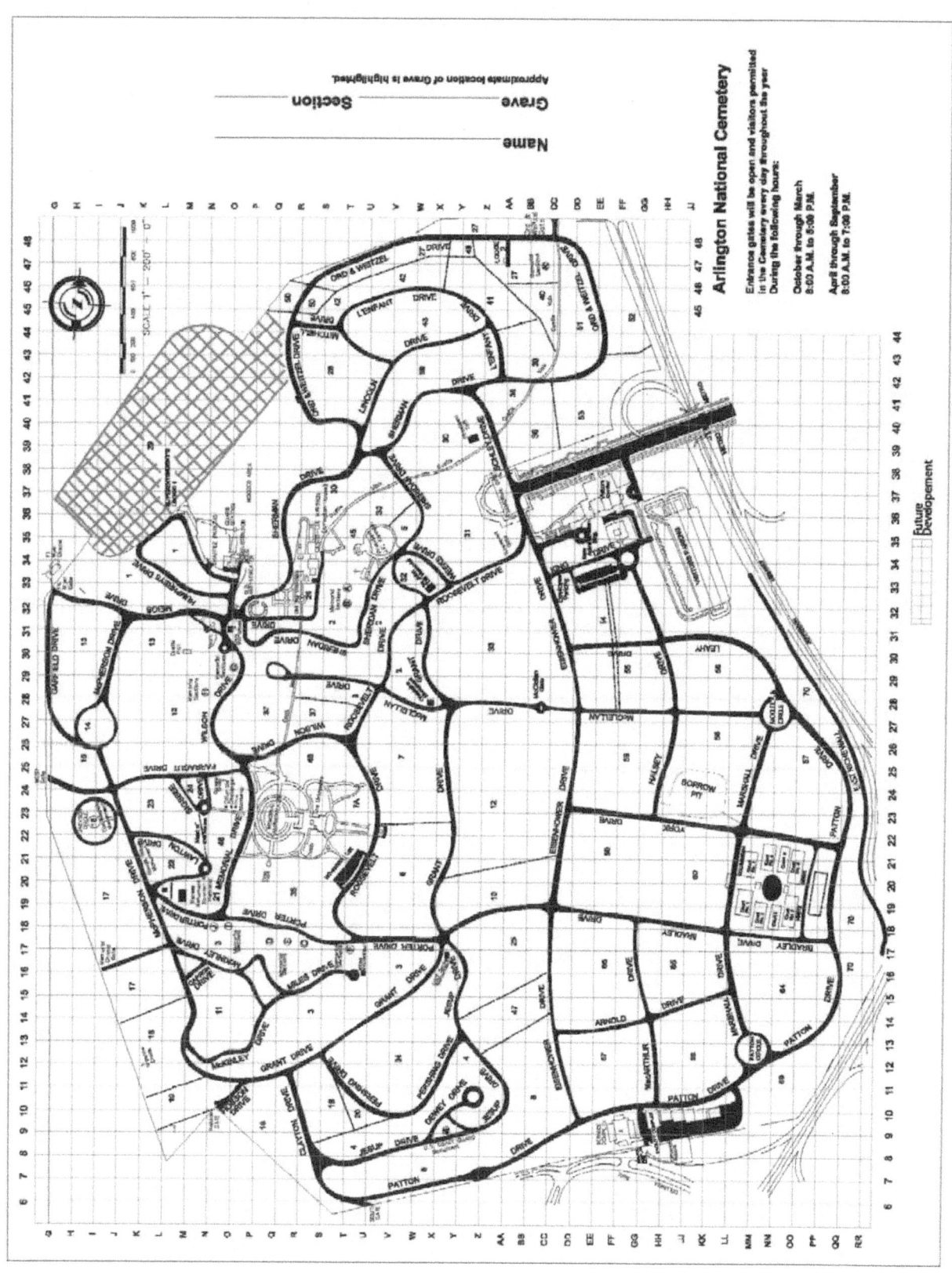

www.ingramcontent.com/pod-product-compliance
Lightning Source LLC
Chambersburg PA
CBHW080735290526
45790CB00008B/3208